The (

L.

PENNÆ PRÆNUMBRA

THE BOOK OF THE
PRE-SHADOWING OF
THE FEATHER

With Commentaries & Elucidation

Scribed by Soror Nema
Edited by Aion 131 & Mike Ingalls

BLACK MOON PUBLISHING
NEW ORLEANS • CINCINNATI
USA

*for the esoteric community in a manner that is unfettered
by commercial considerations.*

Design and layout by
Jo Bounds of Black Moon

This is the compleat edition of *Liber Pennae Praenumbra* as it was received and transcribed by Nema, including a paragraph that was mistakenly omitted from *Maat Magick* published by Weiser in 1995 and an additional paragraph that has been missing since the original publication. This edition also includes additional commentaries and a translation of *LPP* into a simpler and more universal English by Nema.

Special thanks to Oliver Megyesi for discovering a missing paragraph from this edition.

Horus-Maat Lodge art by Peter Carr

ISBN: 978-1-890399-56-6

United States • United Kingdom • Europe • Australia • India

Contents

EDITOR'S INTRODUCTION

Generally it is an editors job to shut up, get out of the way and make whatever changes to the manuscript need to be made to let the voice of the inspired author to be heard in it's clarity. However, I am not just editing this work, I have been profoundly changed in significant ways spiritually, magically, mentally, emotionally and even physically by the book you are about to read. I think few slim texts can make that claim, but *Liber Pennae Praenumbra* has affected thousands of people in just this way. It is not a 'book' in the sense we commonly see books, it is, rather 'a voice from the Akasha' as itself proclaims; a transmission, a significant pronouncement, revelation, instruction manual, talisman and many other things. It is more an EVENT than a thing of paper and ink or electronic symbols.

Liber Pennae Praenumbra has had a profound effect on many luminaries in the occult world, the most famous being Kenneth Grant who discusses and quotes it throughout several of his books. The magickal order I belonged to in the late 1970s, The Grove of the Star & Snake, which was eclectic and open-Thelemic in many ways, took up *Liber Pennae Praenumbra* when it was first published about the same time in *The Cincinnati Journal of Ceremonial Magick*. When read ritually, it lit up our circle like a magickal super nova and we never looked back. In 1979, after massive correspondence, pieces of which ended up in Nema's seminal work *Maat Magick* (Weiser Books) we journeyed to Ohio and our Heru-like energy met and entwined with her Black Flame of Maat and we were directed to form an initiatory vehicle or Order which became manifest as the Horus Maat Lodge. This Lodge is open, universal and can be explored further at horusmaatlodge.com. The Lodge is now 35 years

old and still cooking.

So *Liber Pennae Praenumbra* has been a significant part of mine (and many others) magickal universes and practices for close several decades. The text is, of course, online and it and some commentary are found within *Maat Magick*, the entire Maatian system, but the text, commentaries and *Feathersong* (the adapted text) have never been correlated and published in one place as befits a sacred text, thus this book and my involvement.

Those entering or residing in the esoteric community are likely quite familiar with Crowley, Magick and Thelema as emanating from his received text *Liber Al vel Legis* or *The Book of the Law*. A certain degree of familiarity with his work, especially this last text, may be helpful in understanding the magickal context of the generation of *Liber Pennae Praenumbra*. However, this is beyond the scope of this simple devotional tome. It is likely that if you hold this in your hand, you know what I speak of, so I will simply state that as a Thelemite, I have found working with the Maatian Current and the work embedded in this text to accelerate all other workings and it has helped balance out the sometimes harsh and fiery manifestations of Horus energy, the energy of this aeon of 'force and fire' with a balancing energy and magickal flow that indicates how our species can survive the time of 'force and fire' we are in now (!) and evolve and reach a future of our own devising through the balance and forward momentum of MAAT who was always said to 'guide the course of the sun.'

MAAT tells us clearly that The Great Work of species evolution and of creating a positive and enlightened future is in OUR hands. Quantum physics has confirmed what *Liber Pennae Praenumbra* states, that all times are NOW and that the FUTURE informs the **past** as much as the past and present influence the future. This is the new model; There are many possibility futures, all are real, in several

the Earth is dead or uninhabitable for humans. We can **choose** our species future, the golden thread of our future selves speaks now to us through the voice of MAAT. Will we listen and act? The future is in our hands.

This then is the Great Work.

As Nema always says, "Success to your Work!"

Aion 131
Yule 2015
(Completed Spring Equinox, Full Moon 2016)

"The familiar Egyptian form of the goddess of Justice who is the characterization of the fourth Aeon is Maat. And it was the Aeon of Maat or 'MA-ION' that Crowley's student Frater Achad (Charles Stansfield Jones) later came to advocate as prematurely succeeding that of Horus... [Later] Kenneth Grant [suggested] that Maat was the 'daughter' or complement of Horus the son, and promoted the idea of a 'double current' in which those two god forms [Horus and Maat] were coeval. Probably the most interesting and consequential outgrowth of this premise has been the Maatian magick of Nema, with its own inspired scripture Liber Pennae Penumbra and its independent body of magical technique."

— From *Approaching the Kabbalah of Maat: Altered Trees and the Procession of the Æons* by Don Karr, 2006

THE COMING OF A BOOK

This writing came to me after the vision it describes. It was written in early 1974; I had been introduced to Magick in 1972 through the writings of Aleister Crowley by a friend who called himself Shadow. There was an occult bookshop in the Mt. Adams section of Cincinnati, a shop named the Dawn of Light.

My avid interest in Magick and Initiation led me to spend some time in the DOL, browsing, reading, buying books, conversing with others of like mind who found the shop both haven and meeting ground. Here I met the proprietor, Frater Ariel, and my good friend and Magickal colleague, Frater S.M.Ch.H., who invited me to make use of his private library.

From the crew of would-be magicians who habituated the Dawn of Light arose the proposal for the Cincinnati Chapter of the Crowned and Conquering Child, a group to meet for Working purposes, a fellowship of ritualists to perform group ritual. Frater Ariel's charisma, knowledge, and ownership of the DOL made him the natural leader of the group.

The CCCCC had gathered in the Temple room at Oz farm for a major time-travel Working. There were about 30 of us present, most of whom had links to our previous incarnation in the Alsace-Lorraine region in the 1700's. This night we aimed to push our self-awareness even farther, to a time in pre-history where we were preparing for the destruction of an island nation.

I was one of three voyagers. Fra. S.M.Ch.H. was Master of Ceremonies, Fra. Ariel led the power rhythms of two dozen percussionists, and Shadow was one of the guards. Borne back through time on the tides of the beat, we voyagers called out our

descriptions of scenery, people, and events as we saw them.

Toward the end of our journey narrative, while still surrounded by the perceptions of Level 9 in the past, I became aware of a new presence in the Oz Farm temple in Level 9 in the present. The presence radiated power but threatened no action.

After the ritual was over and the party began, I asked S.M.Ch.H. what he thought of the Working. He said that he had perceived the presence of an extra person in the middle of the rite, and he estimated that the person was a Magus in grade. We speculated that we'd created a vacuum when we ventured pastward, and that the mystery Magus had taken advantage of this vacuum to visit us from our future. We agreed to say nothing of this, and to await further developments.

Two weeks after the ritual I was in the DOL. Fra. Ariel gave me two black feathers, saying, "I don't know why, but I'm supposed to give these to you." I thanked him, and brought the feathers home and placed them on the altar. Two weeks later, I was meditating in both my Level 10 and Level 9 Temples When I heard a voice say, "Call your weapons."

I moved to the altar on Level 9 and called to me the astral bodies of my wand, sword, cup, and pantacle. Holding my weapons/tools, I gazed into the white flame burning about two inches above the center of the astral altar.

A minute speck of black appeared in the heart of the flame, then rapidly expanded until the whole flame burned black, absorbing light. After a moment's pause, the black flame expanded, engulfing the temple and its furnishings. I hung alone in space, galaxies and stars whirling in the vast ringing silence, and the vision began.

— Nema

Liber Pennae Praenumbra

The Book of
The Preshadowing of The Feather

The Black Flame by Nema

Liber Pennae Praenumbra

1. In the Akasha-Echo is this inscribed:

2. By the same mouth, O Mother of the Sun, is the word breathed forth and the nectar received. By the same breath, O Counterweight of the Heart, is the manifest created and destroyed.

3. There is but one gate, though there appear to be nine, Mime-dancer of the Stars. How beautiful thy weft and web, a-shimmering in the fire-dark of space!

4. The two that are nothing salute you, Black Flame that moves Hadit! The less and less One grows, the more and more Pra-NU may manifest. Do thou now speak to us, the children of the time-to-come; declare thy will and grant thy Love to us!

5. THEN SPAKE SHE THAT MOVES:

6. I hurl upon ye, Children of Heru! All ye who love the Law and keep it, keeping Naught unto yourselves, are ye a-blest. Ye have sought the scattered pieces of Our Lord, ceasing never to assemble all that has been. And in the Realm of the Dead have ye begotten from the Dead the Shining One. Ye then gave birth, and nourished Him.

7. Thy Land of Milk shall have the honey also, dropped down

as dew by the Divine Gynander. The pleasure and delight lie in the Working, the Whole surpassing far the Parts together.

8. The Lord of Parts is placed within his kingdom, as done by Beast and Bird. The land of Sun is open but to Children. Heed the Eternal Child — his Way is flowing-free, and suited to the Nature of your being.

9. A Voice crieth in the Crystal Echo:

10.What means this showing-forth? Is Time Itself awry? The Hawk has flown but threescore and ten in His allotted course!

11. She smiles, as beauteous as Night:

12. Behold, He spreads His pinions yet in flight, showering and shaking forth the Golden Light upon the hearts of men. And wherein doth He fly, and by what means? The Feather and the Air are His to ride, to bear him ever in his GO-ing.

13. The pylons of the ages are unshaken, firmly are they Set. The Day of the Hawk has but seen its dawning, and will see its due measure according to the Laws of Time and Space.

14. The Voice then spoke:

15. Then has the Vision failed? Do I behold Thee crookedly, thinking Thee to be Whom Thou art Not?

16. She danced and whirled, scattering starlight in her silent laughter.

17. I Am Whom I appear to be, at times, and then again I wear a triple veil. Be not confused! Above all, Truth prevails.

18. I am the Unconfined. Who is there to say me nay, to say, Thou shalt not pass."? Who indeed may say, Thy time is yet to come," when Time itself is my chief serving-maid, and Space the Major-domo of my Temple?

19. Indeed, O Voice of the Akasha, I am the means by which you speak. By the same mouth that breathes the Air, do words of doubt pour forth. In silence then, do know Me. For I am come with purpose at this time, to aid the Lovers of the Hawk to fly.

The Word of Flight

20. Who falters in the Flight must thereby fall: the greatness of the Gods is in the GO-ing.

21. When first ye fledged, Beloved of Heru, the shell which had protected long had broken. Upon the Wings of Will ye ventured forth, gaining strength and power as ye flew. Ye gained all knowledge of the Feathered Kingdom, whereby ye became as perfect as the Sun. The friends and teachers all became as brothers.

22. The regal Swan, the Heron and the Owl — the Raven and the Cockerel did aid ye. The Beauty of the Hawk Himself was granted, the virtues of the Peacock, the Hummingbird and Loon. The Eagle did reveal her inner nature and the mysteries thereof - behold, ye witnessed how, with her Lion, she became the Swan. And the Ibis of the Abyss did show the Knowledge.

23. Ye flew, O Kings and Hermits! And ye fly even now, within the bending loveliness of NU. But there are those among ye, and below ye, who would snare your wings and drag ye from the sky.

24. Look well within! Judge well your Heart! If ye be pure, it weighs no more than I. It will not bear ye down to the Abyss. For Gold is Light, but Lead is fatal unto flying — plumb your own depths, in Truth and in self-knowledge.

25. If aught would hinder thee, it is thy doing. Behold this teaching now within the Temple.

26. So saying, She-Who-Moves assumed the form of the great Black Flame, growing from the central shaft and billowing out into the Void. The Children of Heru beheld in silence, and listened to Her words form in their hearts.

27. Behold! This lens of Stars now turning in Space before ye — men have named it well Andromeda. Through it I flow unto the holy Moondog, and thence to Ra, and thence to ye, O Priests.

28. Ye must not rest content whilst in the Kingdom, but strive and so exceed in what is done. In Love of the Lady of the North, and in Will of the Prince of the South, do every thing soever. In the power of the Seven-rayed Star do ye comprehend the Beast. And from HAD of the Heart do delight in thy star-arched darling.

29. Do all this, and then, pass beyond. Abandon aught that might distinguish thee from any other thing, yea, or from no-thing. If the fowler would snare thee, leave thy feather-cloak a-dangle in his hand and soar naked and invisible beyond!

30. But now! As priests within the Temple are ye here, as Kings, and Warriors, Magickians all. The Way is in the Work.

31. The Hidden One of the Abyss now gives the two wherein is wrought the higher Alchemy: supporting Earth is Chthonos — learn it well, and all bonds shall be loosed for the Will's Working. Surmounting Spirit, there is Ychronos, whose nature is duration and the passing-away thereof.

32. The two are one, and form the Kingdom's essence. Who masters them is Master of the World. They are the utter keys of Transmutation, and keys of the power of the other Elements.

33. The Warrior-Priests received the Keys, and placed them within their robes, to hold them hidden well above their hearts. The Black Flame danced and dwindled, becoming small, a quill pen, plumed and pointed. There being naught upon which to write, one among the Priests came forth, and laid his body's skin upon the altar as living parchment.

34. She-Who-Moves wrote thereupon a Word, but shew it not before them. In patience waited all the Kings and Hermits, assured full well of final Understanding.

35. The Feather grew again, and rounded close its edges, becoming to their eyes the Yonilingam. The image came of Ancient Baphomet, the Horned One, who spoke:

36. Of old ye knew the Key of Two-in-One conjoined. Ye have lived and loved full measure as NU and HAD, as PAN and BABALON. The Mystery of mine own image do ye also know, for such a Truth

was for the ancient Orders of the East and West.

37. Bipartite has the Race of Man been in its span. The Father and the Mother made a Child. I am the elder of the Children, true — but now the younger rises to His Day.

38. The nature of true Alchemy is that it changes not alone the substance of the Work, but also changes thence the Alchemist. Ye whose Will it is to Work thereby, behold mine inverse image, and consider well its meaning for thy Task.

The Showing of the Image

39. From out of the Yonilingam drifted forth a Cloud, violet and light-shot. In the misty heart thereof a sound arose, vibrating soft, yet filling everywhere.

40. Jeweled and flashing rainbow-lights from wings, there hovered in the midst a humble BEE. Striped gold and brown, soft-haired and curved in form, it shone its eyes unto the Priests and Kings assembled.

41. Spoke then She-Who-Moves from out of the mist surrounding:

42. This is the symbol of the Work-to-come, the Great Gynander in its Earthly form. The Magickian shall grow like unto the BEE as the Aeon unfolds, a leader and sign unto the Race of Man.

43. What then of its nature doth the BEE show forth?

44. Behold, it is not male nor female in the singular. It labors forth by day in constant flight, an egoless do-er, whose will and the Hive

Will are but one.

45. It gathers up the flower-nectar, flies to Hive and there, in pure Comm-Union, doth in its very body Transubstantiate.

46. The Nectar is now Honey. Bee to bee, it is transferred, speaking all Hive Mysteries from and to each mouth. By the same mouth that first ingathered, is the honey spent, the secret Alchemy within the Centers turning Silver—Gold.

47. The Hive now lives, immortal. With queen and workers, drones and builder-bees, soldiers, foster-mothers — all are one. In constant life-renewal, the Hive breathes as One Being — for so indeed it is. In the Will of the Hive is the Will of the Bee fulfilled. Each in its appointed place, the Bees work out their Will in ordered harmony.

48. The image fades. Now the poised Plume moves in dancing fashion, unfolding from the center shaft long wings, transforming to the shape of the dark Vulture.

49. But know, O Children of the Hawk, a Man is not a Bee. He may profit from the image thereof, to learn of Wisdom in the Working. Behold in Me another image for thy heart's instruction.

50. There rose before their eyes the Tower of Silence, wherein the Lovers of Fire lay their dead.

51. The Vulture form alighted soft therein, and ate the flesh from the corpses, to the bone. The wind howled, desolate, in this fearsome place, fluttering the cerements about the ivory bones.

52. Silently, the Winged One stared, gore smeared about her beak. Into the eyes of each Priest there assembled, her baleful gaze did search. In perfect peace they beheld her searching, for each, as Warrior, had made of Death a brother. Deliberately then, she unfolded out her wings, and took to the wind, and soared up from that place.

The Giving of the Word

53. Eternity then reigned, Infinite the veil that hung about them.

54. Somewhere, sometime, the veil parted for a moment, and She-Who-Moves strode forth. More comely than mortal woman ever was, She glowed in radiance of pearl and amethyst. Fine pleated linen was Her gown, girded in gold and silver, and on Her head, a nemyss of starred blue. Her crown was but a single plume, free-standing, and in her hands the Ankh and Wand of healing.

55. Unto each Warrior-Priest she moved, embraced and kissed them. Then, seated in the midst, She spoke as comrade equally-ranked:

56. "All ye who practise well the High Art, hearken. There shall be nothing hidden from thy sight. All formulae and Words shalt thou discover, being initiated by those whose Work it is to aid the Law of Will.

"What was given by Aiwaz is yet unfolding. There is much to do for slaves but newly freed into their Kingship, as ye well know. And each who Works within the Kingdom proceeds space, according to his Will.

57. "Ye have worked well in all that has been given; upon the Tree

of Life are ye founded. In Tetragrammaton have ye proceeded; in all the Beast hath given ye have practised well. Ye have become Hadit, and NU, and Ra-Hoor-Khuit also. As Heru-Pa-Kraath did ye abide in silence. Ye know PAN as lover and as godform, and BABALON is bride and self to you.

58. "The forces of Shaitan have ye engendered, calling forth the nexus of the ninety-three wherein to work your Will. Separation for the joy of Union have ye known, and Alchemy is Science to your Art.

59. "For those who know, and will, and dare, and keep in silence, it goes now further.

60. "In death is Life — for now as ever has it been so. The Willed Death is eternal — keep it so. Self of Ego, selfson born of Maya, must be slain on the moment of birth. The unsleeping Eye must vigil keep, O Warriors, for the illusion is self-generate.

61. "Constant watchfulness is the first Act — the Abyss is crossed by minutes, every day.

62. "If ye would dance the Mask, then mask the Dance. Exquisite must be the Art in this wise; and balance in the Center be maintained, or else ye shall give unwonted Life unto thine own creations. Tread carefully this path of Working, Mage. A tool, by Will devised, makes an ill master.

63. "Now in the Mass, the Eagle must be fed upon what she has shared in making. By the same mouth that roars upon the mountain, is the word-act of No Difference given.

64. "And when Will declares, therein shall join the BEE to add the gold to red and white. The essence of Shaitan is Nectar here, the Temple is the Hive. The Lion is the Flower, now betimes, the Eagle invokes the nature of the BEE.

65. "Within the triple-chambered shrine is the first nectar pooled. The summons of the wand of PAN awakens the portal — opening bliss. And from the third and inmost chamber, in joy supreme, the Sothis-gift, quintessential mead, bounds forth to join Eagle-tears and Lion-blood.

66. "Solve et Coagula. Comm-Union thereby, whereof the Cosmos itself dissolveth, and re-forms by Will. And know, if aught can be so ordered in the Kingdom, that three or more is zero, as well as older truths."

67. Then stirred the Warrior-Priests, and of their number, a nameless one stepped forth.

68. "We know thee, Lady, unspoken though Thy name has been thus far. But say now - what was written on the manskin? What is the word Thou givest?"

69. She smiled and drew from out her robe a parchment scroll, shaped even as a Star. Unrolling it, She turned it roundabout, so all might see.

IPSOS

71. "What is this Word, O Lady — how may it be used?"

72. "In silent wisdom, King and Warrior-Priest. Let the deed shine

forth and let the word be hidden; the deed is lamp enough to veil the face.

73. "It is the word of the twenty-third path, whose number is fifty and six. It is the unspoken Abode, wherein the Dance of the Mask is taught by Me. Tahuti watches without the Ape; I am the Vulture also.

74. "It is the Chalice of Air and Wand of Water, the Sword of Earth and Pantacle of Fire. It is the hourglass and tail-biting serpent. It is the Ganges becoming Ocean, the Way of the Eternal Child.

75. "It names the Source of Mine Own Being — and yours. It is the origin of this sending, that channels through Andromeda and Set. What race of gods do speak to Man, O Willed Ones? The word of them is both the Name and the Fact.

76. "It is for thee mantram and incantation. To speak it is to bring about certain change. Be circumspect in its usage — for if its truth be known abroad, it would perchance drive the slaves to madness and despair.

77. "Only a true Priest-King may know it fully, and stay in balance through his GO-ing flight. This is all I speak for now. The Book of the Preshadowing of the Feather is complete. Do what thou wilt shall be the whole of the Law. Love is the law, love under will."

Donat per Omne Scriba — Nema Sol in Capricornus Anno Heru LXX Cincinnati, Ohio

Beta

Initial Commentary on Liber Pennae Praenumbra

A Comment on Communications
From the Aeon of Maat

Soror ∴.Nema

Originally published in *Cincinnati Journal of Ceremonial Magick* Volume I, Number 2, 1977. Renumbered to coordinate with the texts. —Yule 2015.

Beta is a commentary on the Book of Maat (*Liber Pennae Praenumbra*).

This commentary cannot be completely satisfactory to all. A certain level of background knowledge is assumed; it is inevitable that some will see a belaboring of the obvious, while others will find a great deal of it incomprehensible. To the former, I pray patience; to the latter, I recommend an intensification of study. It will refer to the text according to concepts, although the main referents are sections and paragraphs. To begin:

[The numbers refer to verse numbers (sections) in *Liber Pennae Praenumbra*. —Ed]

2. "By the same mouth" is the first statement of the formula of the Word of the Book. The speech and reception of nectar, creation and destruction, the cycle of Brahma — are conducted

by the same mouth. "Mother of the Sun" — Maat is the Upper Air, wherein rides the Solar Barge of Ra. "Counterweight of the Heart" — the feather is in one pan, the heart of the dead is in the other pan of the scales of Anubis, judge of the dead in the court of Osiris.

3. The "nine gates" are the eyes, ears, nostrils, mouth, anus genitals. The senses and organs of eating, elimination, copulation, and excretion, are one, in that they are the interface between "self" and "Universe".

4. 2=0. The Alchemical formula of Heru produces a Superconsciousness, the Zero. The Black Flame, a contradiction in terms, is the Zen reality that moves Hadit (the observer-point) from Hod to Da'ath, outside the Tree. Pra-NU is Prana, Prakriti and Nuit — the Universe expressed as breath, matter and stars — in short, the Creating Act of Brahma.

Title — "She-That-Moves". Presented as neuter-female motion, Maat's balance is dynamic, not static. She remains upright because of motion.

5-6. This refers to the Isis-Osiris-Horus legend. As the Aeons progress, the Magickian has at his disposal the formulae from previous times in addition to the working formulae of his own incarnation-period.

7. The "promised land of milk and honey" is the outer reference; in addition, the Hindu "Ocean of Milk" or primeval matter, is refered to. The Gynander is the female emphatic of Androgyne. Magickally speaking, there is no difference.

8. The Lord of Parts, Osiris, was installed as King of the Dead by his son, Horus, who is the Bird (Hawk) referred to herein. The Beast is Therion, who superseded the Aeon of Osiris with the Aeon of Horus by the writing of Liber Al. The Kingdom of the Sun is the territory of the Crowned and Conquering Child. The Eternal Child is Lao Tzu, and his way is the Tao.

Dialogue

9-10. Since an AEon supposedly endures for two thousand years, the Voice naturally questions the presence of Maat in the AEon of Heru, which is only seventy years old.

11-19. Her reply indicates that there is no hard-and-fast distinction between these two AEons — that Maat is Heru's vehicle, both as Feather (truth) and Air (prana/life). The course of the ages is well-established by Set/Shaitan.

The triple Veils of Maat are the forms of Isis, Nuit, and **BABALON** — different aspects assumed according to circumstance. Maat is lady of space and time — Prakriti Herself. None can fix limits to her manifestation, since She is the totality of manifestation. The mouth is her instrument — inhalation, exhalation, breath and speech.

The Word of Flight

20 & 21. Gods are not do-ers, but be-ers and go-ers. Balance is maintained by onward motion, such as the balance of the bicyclist, the airplane or the gyroscope. Hesitation, cowardice, indolence, distraction, or diverted direction all lead immediately to the Abyss and a plunge therein.

The brake — the fatal flaw of god-consciousness - is the Egoself. Gods doubt not their powers, nor pride themselves upon their virtues. When Ego transforms into pure forward motion, motion without object or subject, then has the Magickian become a god. When motion is transcended, the Magickian no longer exists, is nothing.

22. The bird-images are according to the Tree of life as follows: The Swan is Kether, as it is a glyph of Aum. The Heron as Chokmah is a symbol of ancient and paternal Wisdom. The Owl denotes Binah, being a bird of night and darkness. Also the connection with Athena is implied, the stern patroness.

The Raven is the bird of Odin, assisting his rulership in Chesed. The Cockerel is a symbol of the warlike nature of Geburah, in terms of duel-to-the-death cockfights. The Hawk, Heru, is Tifhereth. The Peacock is Venus' bird, the singular image for Netzach. The Hummingbird is a type of Mercurial swiftness for Hod. The Loon cries at dusk, and is a dreamlike, haunting factor of Yesod.

The Eagle represents Malkuth in Alchemical workings. In union with the Lion, she resolves Malkuth again into Kether. The Ibis of the Abyss is Thoth, giver of Knowledge to Man, and representing the non-Sephora Da'ath.

23 & 24. The one who snares is the Ego-self. Whether it be the Ego of another or the Ego of the self, the leaden results are the same. One cannot fly as long as one is bound to an identity. The balance of Anubis determines the purity of the heart-the heart versus the feather on the scales. Anything weighing more than Maat. Truth itself, cannot progress nor cross the Abyss.

25. None can restrict the Magickian save himself.

26. The form of the Black Flame, while having overtones of Binah, is the image of the Ain Soph Aur. Black is not, in this case, the absence of light, but the cancellation of it. The radiance and absorption is so finely balanced that the Astral vision percieves black as the color of the Flame. This is limitless light because its operative ecology constantly recycles all radiance without energy-loss. Matter/energy can only be changed, not anihilated.

27. This is the chart of the flow of the ninety-three Current. Maat here declares Herself to be the Current itself — and so She is, in the highest form of Prana. The Andromeda Galaxy is the proximate large-scale focus of the Current: Sirius and Sol are the small-scale foci. The Current's generating origins are not yet stated.

28-29. This is a recapitulation of the godforms of the AEon of Heru. "Passing beyond" indicates the level of consciousness wherein the Magickian transcends the practice of Magick. When one ceases to exist, there is no possibility of "doing" anything. The veil of the "existence" of the Magickian is but an earthing-vehicle for the Current. Ritual may still be performed, but there is no-one performing it; it simply happens.

30-35. Chthonos is matter-energy. Ychronos is time. Together they constitute the space-time continuum, and are reciprocals. The works of Albert Einstein are perhaps the best reference to the nature of this relationship; the Magickian will find himself using these supraelements before completely comprehending

the theories. They are not necessarily amenable to an intellectual approach.

35-38. The remainder of this section is self-explanatory in the light of current historical trends of sexual equality.

The Showing of the Image

39-47. The consciousness of the human race is moving toward the state which will signal the advent of the AEon of Maat. This is a type of Gestalt-Persona, wherein the individuals will share, in addition to their unique consciousnesses, a planet-wide awareness and empathy of being Man. The long-dreamed-of Utopia of the race will manifest soon. There does already exist small instances of this group-consciousness. The gestalts are not yet stabilized in the Kingdom as of this writing. but those working with the Current 93 in proper fashion will have experienced the Gestalt.

48-52. The vulture-image is shown to demonstrate the proportionate nature of Death in this consciousness. The lovers of Fire are the Parsees, descendants of the ancient Zoroastrians.

The Giving of the Word

53-60. Again, a recapitulation of what exists.

61. The reality of the Abyss, the "crossing" of which is a prerequisite of Maat-consciousness, is more textured than the term would imply. Only through the persistent exercise of the total individual Will, can the Abyss be transcended; the illusion of Ego is constantly being regenerated by the play of Nuit. The

initial leap of accepting one's individual non-existence must be followed by continuous acts of death; only when the acceptance becomes an habitual mode of awareness at all times in the waking consciousness can one begin operating in terms of Maat.

62. In operating from the dynamic equipose of Maat, the Magickian achieves mastery of the Compieat Transmutation. He wills the generation of any Ego-mask needed for the Great Work, and employs it with consummate artistry. Only the purely ego-less may achieve the fullness of Maat; and only those firmly centered in Maat may use this technique of Ego-generation safely and successfully.

The ordinary human consciousness needs familiar appearances in another with which to relate and interact. Therefore, the Magickian becomes the needed person at the proper place and time for those the Current directs his way.

The Dance of the Mask begins with the invocation of a suitable godform. From the godform is taken the essence of the Mask, which is then methodically brought down the Tree via each Sephora until it is enriched and balanced with all the subtle nuances of a "Nature-generated" personality. It is then earthed in the Kingdom through action, social intercourse, and acceptance by other "Natural" personalities.

Herein lies the danger: the play of Nuit (or the veils of Maya) are so subtle, persuasive and convincing, that a moment's lapse of control renders the Mask a "reality." Then, the process of Ego-death must begin again... and with greater difficulty, for a perfectly-constructed Ego is much stronger and resistant to destruction than a "Natural". The greater the care and craftsmanship that went into its making, the stronger is its will-to-live. Also, given the nature of the Race of Man, the Ego-

masks that are most effective in changing the consciousness of the "Naturals" tend to lie in the extreme ranges of the illusion of "good" and "evil".

An "evil" Ego-mask is easier to control and recall to non-existence, generally speaking, for the subconscious pressures of the "Naturals" acquainted with it tend to push it into oblivion ... except in cases where the Magickian is working with "Naturals" who are of similar predisposition. A "good" mask receives the subconscious support of its Natural fellows, and thereby requires the utmost delicacy and control on the part of the Magickian. It is advisable not to undertake the Mask of a saint unless there is physical access to one's Magickal peers.

63. A point is made here regarding the Mass of the Holy Ghost, as a preparation for the further instructions regarding the Mass of Maat. Indeed — the M.H.G. is most effectively performed by Magickians of equal ability who share in the Gestalt. The Eagle, having contributed her share of essence in the making of the Elixir, should participate in the consuming of it — otherwise a serious energy-imbalance results. For the Lion to be the only priest in this ritual is nothing more than psychic vampirism.

64-69. Herein is the procedure of the Mass of Maat given. Begin with the statement of Thelema. Banish, then meditate, using the Word of this Book as mantra. This will bring to the conscious minds the reality of bisexuality, regardless of physical form. The Lion becomes lunar, and the Eagle is the active, Solar agent for the first part.

Maat is invoked.

The lion (Air) concentrates prana in the two lower chakras as Eagle (Feather) stimulates his Muladhara centre and receives

the first flowing of the Swadhishatana chakra.

Air rises on the planes. Feather, having received the Nectar, absorbs it at the Anahata chakra and moves it through the Vishuda, Ajna, Sahasrara (where it unites with the Current), down to the Bindu and back through the Anahata. This is repeated, with increasing intensity until the Prana "fountains up" through the Sahasrara and "rains" down through the persona, wherein it collects in the inmost of the triple-chambered-shrine. (The three chambers being vulva, vagina and uterus.)

This pooled Prana is the combination of the initial Prana of Air and the essences of the five upper chakras of Feather. Moreover, by the circular process described above, it is in the utmost distillation, and is the "gold" referred to in the text.

Feather awakens Air in the subtlest manner possible, again assuming the active mode of Nu-Kali. Union follows — the outer release being paralleled by the Pranic union of the Nectar of gold with lion-blood and Eagle-tears.

Following this, Air becomes the Solar agent and Eagle is Lunar. "By the same "mouth" is the Elixir obtained and shared. Some may be left for the charging of talismans, weapons, etc. The most effective mode is in the Moon-time, wherein the added vibrations of chthonos-ychronos are manifest.

Thelema presently operates 2=0. The Mass of Maat uses this in the form 2+x=2/0 wherein the impossible manifests. It is a unisex working; role-reversal is carried to the extent of physiological possibility without resort to artificial implements.

The Elixir is not a simple Alchemical combination, but is a triplicity (x=Maat) and, by extension, infinite.

Dichotomy no longer applies. Energy is now a vector-function of motion, generated by three infinity-sources. Maat, priest and priestess are hermaphrodite-gynanders. By extension and in

varied format, the Maat-working is valid for an individual or a group. The number and type of physical vehicles makes no difference. The homosexual possibilities are obvious.

70-74. IPSOS = "IPSE" + "OS" = "the same mouth."

Experience in its use has varied from the silent mantra-repetition to full-voiced vibration of it. It has moved physical objects when used aloud; in silence, it dissolves the self. It cannot be adequately discussed, only experienced.

75-76. Herein is named the source of the magickal Current, first mentioned as coming through Andromeda. "By the same mouth"... Man is the source. Our children's children, unknown generations hence, the true Magi of the AEon of Maat, are sending us the means of evolution.

They, masters of the space-time continuum, are aiding us to evolve. We also are the children of ourselves. Each time we venture past-wards into the Akasha, our presence effects a consciousness-change in those we observe, especially ourselves in prior incarnations.

Past, present and future are but reference-points in the organic development of the Race. Entropy is a constant, physically, and consciousness-development is its reciprocal.

After we have achieved the race-consciousness, we shall join the Comity of Stars. This is a marvellous Intelligence that has existed from the beginning of this cycle, and shall endure to the end. The youngest members are those planetary races that have achieved global consciousness. There are those whom we see as stars ... plasma-beings whose race-consciousness form the galaxies. There are the absorptive ones whom we percieve as masses of interstellar dust and gas, such as the Horsehead

Nebula. There are those who are willed supernovae, "quasars" neutron-stars, pulsars and "black holes". The ones who are composed of contraterrene matter (reversed atomic charges) were the origins of the concept of the Qlipoth, although their natures are most benign.

These Brethren await our development patiently ... when all sentient beings have achieved complete awareness, we unite, and transcend the space/time continuum entirely. This is the essence of the Boddhisattvic Vow. Those of us who have willed to take the Vow are committed to the furthering of evolution toward this Unity.

77. At the Heat-Death of the Universe, or the Night of Brahma, we will again form the Ylem and allow creation to occur.

The reason for the Dance is the joy thereof ... that, and no more.

TAT TVAM ASI.

Do what thou wilt shall be the whole of the Law; love is the law, love under will.

By the hand of Nema.

[For a more extensive analysis of *Liber Pennae Pennumbra*, see Nema's book *Maat Magick*. —Ed.]

Notes and Comments on Liber Pennae Praenumbra

Nema

(Originally printed in *Maat Magick*)

To save us both unwarranted tedium, I'll only comment on those paragraphs or lines that seem to need it. The numbers refer to the numbered sections in Liber P.P. Please forgive me if I've incorrectly estimated your level of comprehension.

1. The Akasha is the totality of information in our universe, timeless and complete. We can tap into it on all levels if we know how to recognize what we see and know where to look. Sometimes Akashic information arrives in our consciousness uninvited and unannounced; a habit of gentle skepticism helps maintain equilibrium during any resulting chaos.

2. "Mother of the Sun" is Maat's title in Level 3. Traditionally, the Sun travels the ocean of Air from sunrise to sunset in the Barque of Ra. Maat's primary element is Air; her symbol is the feather, her Tarot Trump is Adjustment/Judgement, whose sign is Libra, an Air sign. In Egyptian tradition, Maat is the daughter of Ra, even as she is the Daughter in the IHVH formula.

In the IHVH formula, "the Daughter is placed on the throne of the Mother where she enkindles the Eld of the All-Father." Recently, I've discovered that the displaced Mother is running through the woods, walking invisibly in city streets, having a high old time as the

Grandmother.

Perhaps it is the dethroned Mother who is the key to transcending the IHVH formula. The Father stays with the formula to have his Eld enkindled (the old goat!): the Son has procured the Daughter through redemption for the Father. Tradition doesn't specify if the Son weds the Daughter — we can assume it happens when the Father dies and the Son becomes head of a household and the Kingdom.

The Daughter can look forward to her own eventual liberation as Grandmother, but the Son seems limited to become the Father, then hang on 'til grim death. The IHVH formula needs to be revised for the benefit of the grandfathers — and everyone else.

3. The apparent nine gates are the eyes, ears, nostrils, mouth, genitals, and anus. The true single gate is the mouth, leading to the innermost physical system, the digestive system.

A meditation point. When you really think about our physical form, you'll see we're essentially elaborate donuts, or tori. Through the Magick of complexity and tight folding, the hole of our donut shape is more extensive and elaborate than our skeleto-muscular systems. Our insides are roughly four times longer than our outsides.

From another view, the "Nine Gates" are the senses, and the "One Gate" is our central experiential processor, where data acquire meaning and are woven into their right place in the design of existence. I count the nine senses as: sight, hearing, smell, taste, touch, proprioception, gravitational direction detection, proximity of large objects detection, and awareness of others' attention.

4. The two that are nothing is the formula of 2=0, the essence of sex magic and of Samadhi. Hadit is the irreducible point of view at the center of the universe.

"One" is the initiate. Pra-Nu is prana, prakriti and Nuit. The gist is: the more you absent yourself in your work, the more likely are

universal meanings to cloak themselves in your words and your art and so manifest themselves.

5. She-That-Moves, and, in other places, She-Who-Moves, is the title of Maat in Level 1, or Kether. The "Tree of Maat" is as follows: [I've added Cabalistic Sphere titles. — Ed.]

She Who Moves (Kether)

Mother of the Sun (Binah)   Ongoing Balance (Chokmeh)

(Egg of Heru-Pa-Kraat) (Da'ath)

Air, the Inconfined (Geburah)   Masked Dancer (Chesed)

Black Flame (Tipereth)

Quill Plume (Hod)   Bee Gynander (Netzach)

Maut the Vulture (Yesod)

Black Pearl in the Crystal Lotus (Malkuth)

6. Heru is Horus. The Law is that of Thelema (Greek for "Will"), which reads "Do what thou wilt shall be the whole of the Law; love is the law, love under will." Nought is Nuit-Infinite Space and the Infinite Stars thereof: I.S.I.S.

The children of Heru are addressed as Isis, who collected the pieces of Osiris (corresponding to the Nomes, or districts, in Egypt) after he had been dismembered by their brother Set. Isis conceived Horus with the dead Osiris and raised him in concealment among the reeds in the marshlands of the Nile.

7. The Land of Milk and Honey, the Promised Land, was denied of Moshe, who was also protected by the concealing reeds of the Nile as a child. The "dropping down as dew" refers to the Biblical manna that fed the Israelites in the wilderness.

8. The Lord of Parts is Osiris, placed in his Kingdom of the Underworld, the afterlife, by the Bird, his hawk-headed son of Horus, and the Beast, To Mega Therion, whose *Liber Al vel Legis, the Book of the Law,* marked the end of the Aeon of Osiris and the beginning of the Aeon of Horus.

The Dying God governs the dead. Horus, the Crowned and Conquering Child leads the living.

The Eternal Child is Lao Tzu, and the Way is the Tao Teh King.

10. The Voice says that the Aeon of Horus is only seventy years old, and Aeons are assumed to last 2000 years.

12. She replies that the Aeons of Horus and Maat are running concurrently as a Double Current of Magick. Her natural element of Air and her symbol of the Feather are linked with the hawk aspect of Horus.

13. The Pylons of the Ages are firmly Set, since Set is the Egyptian analog of Saturn, Lord of Time.

14-15. A reference to Crowley's *The Vision and the Voice.*

17. The triple veil refers to trinitary aspects of godforms, such as Maiden, Mother, Crone, and Brahma, Vishnu, Shiva. Truth is Maat.

18. In the Tree of Maat, Air, the Unconfined is her title in Level 5, Geburah.

19. If exercising your freedom of speech created confusion, be

silent and see the truth.

20. This is self-evident to the experienced.

22. The birds are given in their order of densities.

The swan (glyph of Aum) is the light of the Atman; this light is the first layer surrounding Nothing.

The heron, standing on the verge of water and land, is force on the verge of form, Level 2's Logos.

The owl is a bird of night, even as Level 3 is under the Night of Pan.

The raven is a familiar of Odin, who shares in the Jovian nature of Level 4.

The cockerel is a traditional symbol of Martial fierceness in Level 5, as witness the illegal and popular "blood sport" of cock-fighting.

Horus is the hawk in Level 6 as Lord of True Will.

The peacock is associated with various Love Goddesses in Level 7.

Level 8's flash and brilliance of complexity and swiftness is represented by the darting hummingbird.

The loon's cry at evening evokes the moon and the lunar energies of Level 9.

The Eagle is the Alchemical symbol for the female, lunar essence. The Lion is the male, solar symbol. Their union transmutes them into a single entity, the Swan, AUM, the dissolution of Shivadharshana into Nothing; 2=0.

The Ibis of the Abyss is Thoth/Tehuti, divine Scribe and teacher, presiding over Da'ath, the non-Sphere the non-level. Da'ath is both knowledge and confusion, which indicates that knowledge by itself can lead astray without understanding and wisdom to balance it in a trinity.

23. NU or Nuit, is the night sky and neter of the universe. She is

depicted as resting on her feet and hands, her body arched over the Earth. She's a solid deep blue, with stars everywhere in her on her.

Kings and Hermits are the aspects of the Magickian mentioned in Liber Al.

The would-be snarers are anyone or anything that seeks to divert, dissuade, or block you from doing your True Will. One of the greatest snares is to mistake desire-driven attraction for True Will.

24. Lead and gold are both heavy, but lead is poisonous. The Latin word for lead is plumbum.

25. The emphasis is on "doing" rather than on "thy doing." There comes a time when you have to listen to your HGA and allow events to happen through you without editorial comment or trying to do it.

27. The moondog is Sirius. Maat describes part of the route taken by the Magickal Current in the course of its flow. Ra is our sun.

28. Lady of the North: Nuit. Prince of the South: Hadit or Set. The seven-rayed star is the star of **Babalon**; the Beast here is Pan. Hadit and Nuit are referred to a second time.

29. Three pieces of good advice. Pass beyond: we never arrive, since there's no there there. Our business is to go. Distinguish: work for the Vision of No Difference. This is the state in which all things appear equally illusory; no basis for preference can be formed.

Soar naked and invisible: appearances are only that. Where hindrance to True Will appears, install your point of view on the level above it, and resolve matters from the rarer and more comprehensive level.

31. Chthonos is spacetime, matterenergy. Ychronos is the chart of changes that come through the time dimension. Both are fractal

froth complexities.

35-37. The Yonilingam is a stylized statue of the male and female genitals conjoined. It represents the union of male and female principles as the creative force of the universe.

36. **BABALON** is an entity channeled by Aleister Crowley. She is a new godform combining the courage of Joan of Arc, the ferocity of Boudicca, the sexuality of Venus and the rowdiness of a Bacchante. She shares many of the characteristics of Ishtar, and some of the Shakti/Shekina.

Baphomet, or Octinomos, was the alleged "god of the Templars." In the famous image by Eliphas Levi, Baphomet is a goat-headed human figure, seated with drapery in its lap. It has long horns, and a lighted torch rising from the center of its head. Its feet and legs are goatish, hooved and hairy. It has female breasts and an erect phallus. One arm is pointing upward, the other downward; one bears the word "solve," the other, "coagula."

Baphomet is the image of the hermaphodite, the androgyne, the manwoman. Gender has never been as distinct as the mainstream moralists assume, and it's growing less distinct as we go.

42. The worker bee is a neutered female. The hive is a reproductive unit, however, with queens and drones produced at need. The gynander exhibits no sexual characteristics, while the androgyne exhibits all. The gynander's sexuality is concealed and private to itself.

Humanity is not about to abandon sex, but we are in the process of changing it radically. The likeness to the BEE lies in the realm of the developing double consciousness and its effect on global socioeconomics, not in the area of individual sovereignty. "Every

man and every woman is a Star."

49. A Man is not a Bee, even as the map is not the territory.

50. This refers to the followers of Zoroaster, such as the Parsees, who placed their dead in open towers for the vultures. Fire and earth are deemed too sacred for corpse disposal.

54. A nemyss is the Egyptian head cloth that has two lappets hanging below the shoulders on each side of the face.
The Ankh, or crux ansata, is a cross with a loop for the top arm. It represents a sandal strap (the business of the gods is Going) and symbolizes eternal life.
The Wand of Healing is the Caduceus.

56. What was given: Liber AL vel Legis.
Ra-Hoor-Khuit is Horus in his Warrior hawk-form; Heru-Pa-Kraath is Horus as a human infant or child, seated on the lotus and his finger (or thumb) to his lips is the Sign of Silence. The combined form of these two aspects are Heru-Ra-Ha.

57. Shaitan is the Peacock Angel, god of the Yezidis. He is an analog for Set, or Saturn, the traditional Dark Gods. The ninety-three is the Magickal Current of the Aeon of Horus.

59. The Ego is the illusion of identity giving itself undue importance in the scheme of things. Slaying it consists of reminding it or re-demonstrating to the actuality of its status.

60. Crossing the Abyss, or transcending duality, is the essence of Ego-slaying. It needs to be done as a regular practice because the

density of the levels lends credibility to illusion, and we fall back into dualistic thinking and behavior.

61. It's vital to be mindful of the illusions of personality as well as the illusions of Ego. Don't believe your own publicity.

62-65. These are technical instructions for the Mass of Maat, which is described in detail in Level 7 in the Practice Section.

68-69. IPSOS is the Word of the Aeon of Maat. It had four pronunciations and nine spellings. (This information is probably of more interest to the Gematrist than to others.) The four pronunciations are: IPSOS, IPSOSh, IPShOS, IPShOSh. Among other things, these four pronunciations do interesting things in pranayama meditation: IPSOS-inhale, IPSOSh-hold, IPShOS-exhale, IPShOSh-hold. Again, for the Gematrist:

I -	10	10	10	10	10	10	10	10	10
P -	80	80	80	80	80	80	80	80	80
S -	60	60	300	60	60	300	60	60	300
O -	6	6	6	70	70	70	X	X	X
S -	60	300	300	60	300	300	60	300	300
	216	456	696	280	520	760	210	450	690

The significant Thelemic numbers I've used investigating these numerations are: 11, 31, 56, 93, 111, 131,156, 333, 418, 666, and 718. The numer 123 = EHEIHE IHVH ALHIM, implying Kether, Chokmah and Binah.

(216) – 93 = 123. Also, (456) – 333 = 123.

123 + 111 = 234 + 111 = 345 + 111 =

(456) + 111 = 567 + 111 = 678 + 111 = 789.

(456) + 333 = 789. Also, (696) + 93 = 789.

780/3 = 263 = Gematria

678/6 = 113 = the same as in "the same mouth."

567/21 = 27. 21 = Existence, 27 = Purity

(456)/8 = 57 = consuming (re. mouth), wealth, subversion.

345/5 = 63. Also 567/9 = 63. 63 = fed (re. mouth).

234/13 = 18. 13 = love, unity.

18 = chai (life) my beloved.

(456) – 93 = 363 + 333 = (696). (216) + (450) = 666.

(280) – 156 = 124 = 93 + 31.

(216) – 131 = 85 = Pe = Mouth (as Pe spelled in full.)

(456) – (216) = 240 + (456) =

(696) – (216) = 480 + (280) = (760).

480/2 = 240. 480 + 240 = 720.

720 = 9 x 80. 80 = Pe = Mouth.

At this point we'll have mercy on those who have no acquaintance with or interest in the play of numbers.

70. This refers to the Hermit card in the Thoth Deck, recalling Diogenes' search for an honest man. A Word of Power is not to be squandered on the street, where it wouldn't be understood and where its power would be dissipated. Show is stronger than tell; let the Word manifest itself through you and your art as fact.

71. There are twenty-two paths on the Tree of Life, traditionally. Fifty-six is the number of NU. The Ape of Thoth is an ape sacred to the god; it's also the imitation of teaching, science, knowledge or Magick. The Vulture is Maut, dark image of immaculate conception, whose mate is the southwest wind.

72. The attributes of the elemental weapons are traded around. The hourglass is time and the tail-biting serpent (Orouboros) is eternity.

73. The source of Maat's being, and ours, is the same mouth, our own mouth, mouth of womb and tomb, mouth of river and cave. The Word creates the mouth by which it is spoken, dilating a doorway in the nothingness, then stepping through it. Meaning, information, and significance are inherent in the structure of the cosmos in all its levels. There is only one thing, and it's very busy. As space and time expand, it gets busier spinning itself into more complexities.

The complexities outpace the expansion 2 to 1 in exponential quantum increments.

This requires intricate folding and coiling (like our cerebrum and intestines), curving into fractal froth, generating complexities and connections among them. The one thing is being everywhere simultaneously, creating space as it jumps beyond the previous

points in all directions from its initial point.

The wind of its passage stirs the complexities, sets them rotating. The inevitable collisions of points, lines, and sections generate points of mass which drop below light speed and take up the trade of quarks. The plunge of mass into subluminal life generates energy which follows the path of the plunge, a subluminal energy.

We are composed of this one thing; its laws apply to us, in translation, from the superluminal to the subluminal. "That which is above is like that which is below; that which is below is like that which is above." We are essentially hardwired to understand ourselves and the Cosmos, sub- and super-luminary.

Our lack of understanding arises from our prolonged transition from our pre-hom ancestors to the mature and united consciousness of N'Aton. Mind is clouded and impeded by emotions, urges, hormones, and wrong ideas. N'Aton uses the superluminary realm to travel back to us, to give us the concepts and ritual tools we need to speed up the process of our becoming N'Aton.

The Magickal Current originates in the essence of things. As a species, we've been broadcasting our signature to the cosmos since the invention of speech. Since the advent of radio and television, our signal has gained much more power.

Our signature signal returns to us through the galactic lens of Andromeda, augmented and aimed by the Sirius system, and stepped down by our sun. The returning signal is changed by its journey, shaped by the cosmos, augmented by stellar energy and enriched by the information gained from our intelligences.

74. The masses of people faithful to the mainstream religions will not welcome the implications of IPSOS for a number of reasons.

There was no fall from grace, no Original Sin, no lost preternatural gifts. "If ignorance were bliss, 'tis folly to be wise." The garden of

Eden was our pre-human animal consciousness, too primitive for moral distinctions, too simple for guilt, innocent of the capacity for sin.

We emerged in the animal kingdom as the most neurologically complex species on the planet; we have not fulfilled the responsibility of this fact. Our development has been uneven. Our science and technology have outdistanced our wisdom, and we pay for this imbalance with the doing of evil and suffering for and from it.

In a sense, we have lost the grace of acting with Tao through the overwhelmingly intimate influence of urges misunderstood and misapplied. No individuality, divine or otherwise, can redeem us individually or collectively. No dying and resurrected divine incarnation can restore us to the grace of seeing God.

Only we can transform ourselves through initiation and hard work. When we learn to cooperate with the nature of things, when we learn to see and understand the nature of things, when we expand our sense of self to include the cosmos, then and only then, will we attain the innocence of living in wisdom. Our grace is that of seeing God in the Universal Pattern of Consciousness and its Divine Intelligence in which we participate.

Maat Magick suggests the term "sacred humanism" for seeing the perfectibility of mankind and working toward that perfection. Individually and as a species, we are not a finished product, nor a fully conscious one.

We invent gods to explain to ourselves the mysteries of life; we invent heaven as a compensation for earthly misfortunes and pain. We invent hell as a similar compensation, one often tinged with vengeance and moral self-righteousness. We invent Satan as an excuse for violating our own ethics, as a tempter responsible for our own leanings to sin.

IPSOS implies the need for a spiritual maturity wherein we become

our own heroes, saints, and gods, shouldering the responsibility of our own salvation without benefit of clergy, church, or priesthood.

75. Each Magickian is to function as a Priest, not as an intermediary, but as friend, mentor and advisor. Each Magickian is to function as a King; not as one commanding, but as caretaker of one's sphere of influence and those living within it.

FEATHERSONG
A Restating of Liber Pennae Praenumbra

Note by Nema:

I've written a number of commentaries on *Liber Pennae Praenumbra* over the years, attempting to explain the more obscure words and passages of its specialized language and spirit. As a received document, the information was forced into its manifested form by my own shortcomings, by my lack of experience, and by my immersion in the Victorian/King James Bible style of the writings of Aleister Crowley.

This time, I was inspired to translate it into a simpler and more universal, English. This serves the purpose of a commentary, in my opinion. Even in the simpler language I've found myself writing in poetic meter and occasional rhyme, but this seems proper to the subject matter. I've chosen not to use a Latin title for this new look at an eternal subject; I call it FEATHERSONG.

1. These words rise from eternity:

2. Lady of air, upon which sails the sun-god's boat, the same mouth speaks and drinks. Lady of spiritual balance, the same mouth creates and devours.

3. All means of our linking with the world through perception, nourishment, and love, can be symbolized in and by the mouth. Your cosmos is so beautiful!

4. All lovers lost in each other salute you, light beyond human sight, whose nature can change the inner self. As the sense of self diminishes, the flow of cosmic energy through one increases. Tell us, the children of the future, what you desire. Tell us of your love.

5. Speaks the balance of motion:

6. I fly to you, you who do your will. Blessed are you who love under will and who give all of yourself to the universe. As Isis gathered the pieces of Osiris' body, so you pursue your history. By understanding the past, you conceive the vision of what mankind should be. You work to bring this vision to actuality.

7. The future you seek to manifest will sustain and pleasure you, when men and women war no more. Working to transcend your present state brings joy; those working together to transcend will be more successful than many working individually.

8. The institutions of control belong to the past; the twentieth century has seen the rise of individual freedom and responsibility. The future belongs to the innocent and the open minded, to those who live gladly in the flow of things.

9. The scribe, as self-appointed critic and representative for humanity, speaks:

10. What are these words? An Aeon is supposed to last two‹ thousand years. The era of spiritual and political submission just ended in this century with its birth of the spirit of individual sovereignty. This spirit has just begun its work.

11. The Lady is amused, but kind.

12. The spirit of the new age, like a hunting hawk, still flies in the sun, enlightening and encouraging those who watch and love him. But how does this hawk fly? By the air (and I am Lady of the air) and by the feathers of his wings (and the feather is my special symbol).

13. Time is as stable as it ever was, and history within it, implacable as Saturn/Set, the Lord of time and necessity. The hero-hawk will fly for as long as his work remains the death of restriction and servility.

14. Again, the scribe:

15. Am I mistaken, then to think your Aeon is to follow his? Are you not Maat?

16. Again, the Lady is amused.

17. At times you see me as truth personified; at other times I can be seen as maiden, mother, and crone, or as the veils of nothing, limitlessness and limitless light. Do not confuse yourself in my varied appearances; truth rules.

18. I cannot be caged. Who can bar my way or stop my advent when time and space are my own servants?

19. In fact, scribe, you need me to speak. The same mouth that breathes my air gives voice to doubts. Know me in silence, come to further enlighten the doers of will.

The Word of Flight

20. Your balance is maintained by forward motion; never tell yourself that you've arrived.

21. When you abandoned old ways of control, their institutions were already dying. In your questings for the truth you've found a resonance in symbols of the birds.

22. Crowned in silence on a starry sea,
   serenely glides the Swan, forever free.

   Balanced on one foot where sea meets shore,
   the Heron ponders wisdom evermore.

   The great eyes of the Owl can understand
   the ways of hunting in a night-dark land.

   The Raven's call for mercy must be heard
   in honor of the ebon battle-bird.

   With strength of trumpets in his greeting cry,
   the Cockerel hails light in eastern sky.

   Soaring in the sunrise, beauty-bright,
   the Hawk enraptures all who see his flight.
   In victory the Peacock spreads his fan,
   a thousand eyes of love he shows to man.

Swift as thought and splendid as a flower,
the Hummingbird's a flying jewel of power.

The dreamers heed the haunting call of Loon,
founded in the dusk of mist and moon.

Beneath her wings the Eagle's kingdom flows,
as to her mystic lover Lion she goes.

Alchemic union changes her to Swan--
with realm and crown conjoined she travels on.

The Ibis on the verge of starless deeps
unveils the secret knowledge that he keeps.

23. From them you learned to fly, my noble souls, as you fly now within the sea of stars. Beware of danger, though, from traitors and from those who envy you, who would abort your flight.

24. Contemplate your heart and judge yourself. If you are honest, your heart weighs no more than does my feather-form. It will not pull you down the starless deeps. Alchemic gold is light, but inert lead of unjust deeds will bind you to the ground. Search deeply for your inner nature.

25. If anything would hinder you, it is your doing; let action do itself. See this teaching now within the Temple.

26. So saying, the balance of motion assumed the appearance of the great Black Flame, the light beyond sight, growing from

the feather-shaft and billowing out into the Void. The doers of will watched silently, and listened to her words form in their hearts.

27. Look well! This lens of stars, this galaxy, is the one named Andromeda. Through it, I, the balance of motion, the Magickal Current, flow to the Sirius system, then to your Sun, then to your individual selves.

28. The work of transformation lasts a lifetime. In cosmic love and innate will do everything. Through compassion understand your primal self. From the center of your self embrace the universe.

29. Do this, then go farther. Lose all that is not you, that separates your essence from the ineffable. If anything or anyone would capture you, leave the part they grasp, like empty clothing, a naked soul.

30. Now you gather in our sacred space, as guides of the spiritually hungry, as doers of will, as defenders of truth, as changers of manifestations. The flow of things, the Tao, the truth, is found in transformations.

31. The Ibis-headed Thoth, cosmic scribe and Lord of science, gives the basic keys of world and spirit. Chthonos underlies matter-energy; learn its essence, control its power. Ychronos is true eternity, in which lies time and the dimensions beyond it.

32. These two keys are one, the essence of the physical world. They are the keys of transmutation and of the power of the elements.

33. The assembly received the keys, taking them to heart. The Black Flame danced and dwindled, becoming a quill-pen. There being nothing on which to write, one of the assembly laid his body's skin upon the altar as a living parchment. (In visions are great wonders, as in dreams.)

34. The Lady wrote on it a word, but did not show it to them. In patience the gathering did wait, knowing that in time they'd have the word.

35. Again the quill-pen grew, taking on the form of the Yonilingam. From this sign of male and female unity arose the image of Baphomet, who spoke:

36. You know the secrets of sexual Alchemy. You've lived and loved as universe and self, as Nature's Lord and Lady of willed love. You also know my nature, the androgyne, hermaphroditic archetype.

37. Two main genders has the human race; the man and woman generate the child. I am the older of the children, containing beast and human, male and female. My younger brother, human Horus, charismatic warrior, enlightens now the world.

38. True Alchemy, in changing substances through love, changes also the Alchemists. If you would work this way, learn from my sister-opposite.

THE SHOWING OF THE IMAGE

39. From the Yonilingam rose a cloud of sparkling violet, from which came a soft vibration.

40. Striped in amber and burnt umber,
   eyes of jewels, rainbow wings,
   as you hover, so we wonder,
   loving honey, fearing stings.

41. The Lady's voice rings from the violet cloud:

42. This is a symbol of your future's Work. Take note of how‹ the Bee suggests a way of living suited to large human numbers.

43. In what ways does the Bee's nature teach us?

44. The worker bee is neither male nor female, even though it's female in its form. For all its life its joy is in the hive; it labors for the benefit of all.

45. Flower to flower does it fly, nectar drinker, pollen captor, then to hive. Within its body, it changes nectar's nature.

46. The nectar is now honey, circulating to and from each mouth. In the taste of message molecules, each bee knows the state and health of all. By the same mouth that gathered up the nectar, is the honey spent. In process and in circulation then, does food become an information chain.

47. The hive's alive, a being in itself, immortal as a bee sees it, and home. Queen and larva, nurse and guard, honey bringer, builder of the comb, old one fanning wings in doorway wait the fatal bridal flight of drone. In the will of the hive is the will of the bee fulfilled. The task of each age is where the bee finds joy.

48. The image fades. The Black Flame-feather dances, growing

wings, becoming the dark vulture.

49. But be aware, you who do your will, a man is not a bee. Humans can profit from Nature's examples, but never take a metaphor too far. Watch me for another image.

50. A vision rose—the Tower of Silence where the Parsees lay their dead. The fire and the earth, too sacred for a corpse, bade them offer such to air and bird.

51. The vulture lit upon the Tower and ate the flesh from corpses, to the bone. The wind howled, desolate, fluttering the corpse-cloth about the ivory bones.

52. Into the eyes of each of the assembly the blood-stained vulture stared. They each returned her gaze in peaceful silence. None of them feared death; each had embraced it. The vulture spread her wings, took to the wind, and soared up from the Tower.

The Giving of the Word

53. Eternal, infinite, a veil enclosed them.

54. Time began again as the veil parted;
    infinity became a woman's form.
    More beautiful she was than mortal woman;
    her light of amethyst and pearl shone warm.
    Her gown was made of fine Egyptian linen,
    about her waist were wings of silver-gold.
    Her headdress, midnight blue with stars of diamond,
    a circlet and her single plume did hold.

In one hand was the Ankh, the crux ansata
the sandal-strap of gods who live to Go.
The other held a wand of woven serpents,
the healing-rod of Thoth from long ago.

55. She moved among the gathered seekers, embraced and kissed each one. She sat with them and spoke as though with equals.

56. Listen to me, mages; hear me, sages. Nothing will be hidden from your sight. All patterns of rites and words of power will be yours. Heed the counsel of your elders on the path.

57. You've done well in your learning. You understand the Tree of Life and its Qaballah; you comprehend the Tetragrammaton. You know willed love and how to use its power. You have become the secret Self, and Cosmos, and Horus, warrior of will. As Harpocrat, you kept yourself in silence.

You've loved Pan and you've been Pan; you've loved and been the Lady Babalon.

58. You've raised and used the darker powers of Set-Shaitan-Saturn-Shiva, to link with Horus in the work of will. You've seen yourself as separate from the cosmos so in your union with it you find joy. Experiments in mind and body point the way for creativity.

59. There's more to learn, my noble souls, even as you know, and will, and dare, and keep in silence.

60. In death is life, as nature's cycles show us. Deliberated

death of self's illusion takes you out of time; continue this. The self of ego, this illusion of identity, must die each time it forms. Be vigilant, since this illusion generates itself.

61. Keep a constant watch—the Abyss is crossed by minutes, every day.

62. If you would dance the Mask, then mask the Dance. Your art must excel in making selves to fit your audience, be it human, Other, or you, yourself. Your natural self's unreal, the Masks are even less. Maintain a dancing balance in their making, lest they convince you they contain your essence. A tool, devised by will, makes a bad master.

63. In Alchemy are partners equal, the lunar Eagle and the solar Lion. By the same mouth roaring on the mountain is this equity acknowledged.

64. When you choose, invoke the Bee to join its golden sacrament of hive to Lion's red of male and Eagle's white of female. Nectar is the seed, the temple-hive's the womb, the nectar is the Lion's and the Eagle acts as Bee.

65. Within her heart and self this gathered nectar fountains up and pools. Then Lion rises, summoning new bliss. And from the third and inmost temple-chamber flows the charged nectar, golden mead, to join the Eagle's tears and Lion's blood.

66. Dissolve in the selflessness of psychic death and then reform as will and work requires, in rebirth more than resurrection. This is the sacrament by which the Cosmos dissolves and reforms by

will. And know, upon the plane of earth, that three or more is zero, as well as other truths.

67. The assembled ones then stirred, and from their ranks a nameless one stepped forward.

68. We know you, Lady, unspoken though your name has been thus far. But say now — what was written on the manskin? What is this word you give?

69. She smiled, and drew from her robe a parchment scroll shaped as a star (for every man and every woman is a star). Unrolling it, she turned it roundabout, so all might see.

IPSOS

70. What is the word, O Lady — how may it be used?

71. In silent wisdom, noble soul. Let the deed shine forth and let the word be hidden; the deed is lamp enough to veil the face.

72. It is the word of the twenty-third path that leads beyond the Tree. Its number is given as fifty-six, the day of dread beauty to come when everything changes. It is the unspoken abode, where I whisper its dance of the Mask. Tehuti keeps watch with his Ape, recording without opinion.
   I am the vulture also, sharing the prey of the hawk.

73. It is the Chalice of Air and Wand of Water, the Sword of Earth and Pantacle of fire. In it are contradictions reconciled.
   It is the hourglass and the tail-biting serpent, Ouroboros, mighty in time and in eternity. It is the Ganges becoming ocean,

the Way of the Eternal Child, which is the Tao of Lao Tze.

74. It names my source and yours. It is the origin of this sending, which flows through Andromeda and Sirius. What race of gods speak to mankind, my willed ones? The word of them is both the Name and Fact.

75. It is for you mantram and incantation. To speak it is to bring certain change. Take care in using it. If its truth be widely known at this time, it could drive the sleepers to madness and despair.

77. Only the awakened can understand it fully and use it wisely. This is all I speak for now. The Book of the Preshadowing of the Feather is complete.

Do what thou wilt shall be the whole of the Law.
Love is the law, love under will.

Given through All.
Written by Nema.

Sun in Capricorn, 1974 ce
Cincinnati, Ohio

POSTSCRIPT

The Evolution of Maat Magick:
from Cornfields to Cyberspace

Maat is the principle, or neter, of truth, justice, balance and honesty, personified as a young woman wearing a feather tucked into her head-band. She is sometimes depicted as a feather occupying a balance-pan of the scale in the judgement hall of Osiris, a scale used for the weighing of the heart of deceased. She is the daughter of Ra, and the wife of Tehuti.

Maat Magick is a Thelemic system of self-initiation, founded on the principles of Aleister Crowley's writings. There are differences in the details of the systems, though, adaptations to the technological breakthroughs, political changes, scientific discoveries and further visionary experiences of the past century.

One major difference lies in the concept of Aeons. The godforms for whom Aeons are named reflect, in their natures, the general imagery, or formulae, of the prevalent society of their times. Crowley saw the Aeons in sequence; I see them in parallel. The Aeon of Maat is not a replacement for the Aeon of Horus, but operates in concurrence with it. Likewise, the Aeons of Isis and Osiris are still in practice and in belief in various locations around the world.

I use the Aeon of Bes as the Nameless/ancestral Aeon, extending backward in the timestream. The Aeon of Harpocrat is the Wordless/descendants' Aeon, extending forward into the future. You can order Aeons in the number and formation that best suit your needs, to the extent of your understanding of them. I began by thinking that

Horus and Maat comprised "the double current", but accumulating experiences showed me that Maat Magick is a Panaeonic Magick.

Thus a concept evolved within an evolving system.

Maat Magick was created from the empty spaces around the works of Aleister Crowley on the shelves of an 'occult' shop called "The Dawn of Light". In the early 1970s, there were a few books by Israel Regardie, Dion Fortune, Frater Achad and Kenneth Grant, but none of the range of works that I'd expected to find.

Crowley had written, I thought, that Magickians were supposed to discover their own systems of Magick, not to depend on his writings alone for their Initiations. The discovery of one's own Magick, and the successful practice of it, seemed to me to warrant publication of it, if for no other reason than to share information with one's colleagues. Where were the books?

Imagine a world without the Internet and its foremost search engine prophet, Google. Except for the small band of like-minded seekers to be encountered at the occult shop, I could only presume that there were seekers in other places around the world. At the time, all I could do as a beginner in the High Art was to open myself to the service of whatever idea or entity that was searching for a means of expression.

After a series of events and improbabilities, I had a vision, complete with voice-overs, that was written as *Liber Pennae Praenumbra: The Book of the Foreshadowing of the Feather*. Since incoming information is framed in the vocabulary of the receiver, and since I was immersed in Crowley's writings at the time, Liber PP's language resembles his in style — which I call King James biblical. I've since updated it as a longish poem named *Feathersong*. Liber PP appears in each of two books: *Maat Magick: a Guide to Self-Initiation*, and *The Way of Mystery: Magick, Mysticism & Self-Transcendence*. *Feathersong* is only in *The Way of Mystery*.

Another factor in the early development of Maat Magick was an entity called N'Aton. N'Aton appears as an androgynous human, with golden skin, hair and eyes and his right side is always in shadow. The shadow contains different things on different occasions: a crowd of human faces, a star-filled night sky, symbols, aliens, and so on.

Who or what is N'Aton? Before I attempt a definition, I ask you to suspend disbelief in the relative realities this definition requires.

N'Aton is the shadowy uninvited participant that manifested during a group time-travel Working. Only three of about thirty ritualists saw or felt the presence of this guest, as far as I know. We (Louis Martinié, Herb Zigler, and I) decided to keep silent about it in order to avoid influencing others. No one else from the group has come forward so far with any such report.

N'Aton is the tour guide who showed me the multiverse and its probability-worlds, where our Mainstream Reality traces a glowing trail of manifestation that we call "history" among linked choice nodes. I met interesting life-forms in environments deadly to humans, and saw the paths leading to various futures for our species and our planet.

N'Aton is the persona of the emerging Homo veritas, which differs from Homo sapiens in that people have a double consciousness: that of their individuality and that of the whole species. It can be viewed as Jung's "Racial Unconscious" becoming "Racial Consciousness". Through a field effect of empathy and telepathy, I can literally feel your pain, you can feel mine, and we both can link with large numbers of others who know how to teach us effective pain management. We filter the input of this 'telempathic' sense in much the same way our familiar physical senses edit the teeming world for our consideration. Total immersion in the species consciousness is relatively rare, but the global network of human consciousness is available at all times.

N'Aton sleeps in most of us, but is waking up, stretching and

yawning, in some of us. N'Aton is us, and our children, and our new incarnations, and also those ancestors of ours who lived in wisdom, and helped our species survive and change. I was informed, in the course of cosmic tours, that a simple majority of humans, when awakened to our species-consciousness, will pull the rest along with us.

N'Aton isn't a godform in the classical sense of the word, although he/she/we might be regarded as such by mages in the devotional stage of Initiation. N'Aton is a metaperson, and is our genus' representative among other living beings.

In 1976, Louis Martinié and his small group named Bate Cabal published the first issue of *Cincinnati Journal of Ceremonial Magick* which contained *Liber Pennae Praenumbra*. Subsequent issues carried more writings on Maat Magick, which generated a number of letters to the magazine. The most memorable letter was from a group of young Thelemic Magickians and fellow members of the Typhonian Order from New York City, the Grove of the Star and the Snake. They wrote to say that the material they'd read was useful in their own practices, and that they wanted to visit me for a weekend.

They drove out to the Maat-Pangrove Abbey of Thelema, a farmhouse and barn on ten acres of land in Brown County, Ohio, where I lived with my children, my brother and his lady, and a floating roster of visitors. Two days and a night of intense rituals saw the birth of the Horus-Maat Lodge, whose charter we signed November 25, 1978. The first day of ritual was dedicated to Horus, a sunny day in the cornfields; the second day was misty and cloudy, and we invoked Maat in the woods at the back of the property. The night was rainy for a rite of rebirth. Four of the founding members remain active in the HML: Fra. Aion, Fra. Shade, Fra. Nemus, and I.

The HML continued to grow through private correspondence, a newsletter called *The Hermetic Expedient*, and periodicals like

Mandragore, Aeon, and the *CJCM.* The generous support of Kenneth Grant, particularly in his books *Nightside of Eden* and *Outside the Circles of Time*, introduced the idea of Maat Magick to his global readership. More importantly to me, Mr. Grant's interest and generosity encouraged me to persevere in Magick despite rough patches in the course of Initiations.

In 1980, 1981 and 1982, the Abbey hosted the Warrior Lord Workings, gatherings of about 30-40 Magickians, to read the three chapters of Liber AL in a ritual setting, hold lectures and workshops, display artworks, and engage in long, esoteric discussions.

In 1983, while riding home from work, I heard a silent but sonorous voice telling me "The thrones must be filled". This statement was repeated several times. Some channeled materials arrive with sound and sights, some arrive as unlearned knowledge. Following the voice came the understanding that filling the thrones meant filling the catena of Initiation, which in turn meant there should manifest at least one person for every Sephira. These Throne-holders should work toward, and attain, the understanding and wisdom of their particular Sephira; each should then emanate the essence of his or her Sephira/Throne to the world. This would hasten human spiritual/ psychic evolution in preparation for the double consciousness to come.

Da'ath was to be included. There was given a group rite to send out a call for Throne-holders. The project is called the Elevenstar Working. The ritual was first performed at Winterstar in 1984. The Winterstar Symposium is held every February by the Association for Consciousness Exploration, or ACE, based in Cleveland Ohio.

The Elevenstar rite was also performed in Seattle, Washington, as part of a celebration of the Harmonic Convergence in 1985. Maat Magick was published in 1985, and I received a number of letters commenting on its usefulness to the practice of various types and

traditions of Magick.

During this time, I was corresponding with a number of people living in Great Britain and on the Continent, who came to form the European Maat Network. In 1990, my husband Mike and I had the pleasure of flying to England to meet with various colleagues, to visit Stonehenge, Avebury, Oxford (where I'd been invited to lecture), Brighton and other locations, and to hold a mighty ritual at Silbury Hill on Lammas, the first of August.

The following decade was filled with lecture-workshops at the ACE Winterstar Symposia in spring and at Starwood gatherings in summer. Book signings were usually accompanied by lecture-workshops, and these were held in Columbus and Cincinnati OH, Seattle WA, Portland OR, New Orleans, LA, New Paltz NY, and in other cities in the US. During this time I was working on *The Way of Mystery*, and on art for the *Maat Tarot* (still in slow progress).

In July of 1999, Fra. Aion put the early documents of the Lodge online; the response was such that we currently have 116 members worldwide. We communicate on an email list, which has but one rule: no flaming.

We've adapted the Elevenstar rite for internet use as follows:

Every new moon, participants meet astrally at Moonbase Temple, situated in the center of the visible face of our satellite, while acting in our individual temples physically. We discuss and agree upon a word of power, an image and a sigil a few days in advance, then employ these in rites of individual devising. We send our Magical Records of the ritual to the HML list during the following few days.

During the first five years the Elevenstar Working served as a means of self-initiation for the membership. This year, we're making astral contact with successive age groups of the human race. Thus far we've covered the pre-born to age 1, 1 to 7 years, 7 to 14, and our next new moon, that of April 2004, will focus on the 14 to 21 year group.

If you're interested in viewing the Horus Maat Lodge website, go to horusmaatlodge.com.

The latest venture, brought to manifestation by Frater Aion, is the Silver Star online magazine. Its URL is horusmaatlodge.com/silverstar.

In the time remaining to me in this presentation, I would like to read for you an updated version of *Liber Pennae Praenumbra*. It's in contemporary English; I've named it *Feathersong*. [In this book. —Ed]

— Nema

Text of lecture delivered 4/10/04 at the Thelemic Conference held at Conway Hall, London.

Liber Pennae Praenumbra

In the Akasha-Echo is this enscribed:

By the same mouth, O Mother of the Sun, is the word breathed forth and the nectar received. By the same breath, O Counter-weight of the Heart, is the manifest created and destroyed.

There is but one gate, though there appear to be nine, Mime-dancer of the Stars. How beautiful thy weft and web, a-shimmering in the fire-dark of space!

The two that are nothing salute you, Black Flame that moves Hadit! The less and less One grows, the more and more Pra-Nu may manifest. Do thou now speak to us, the children of the time-to-come; declare thy Will and grant thy Love to us!

Then spake She-That-Moves:

I hurl upon ye, children of Heru! All ye who love the Law and keep it, keeping Nought unto yourselves, are ye a-blest. Ye have sought the scattered pieces of Our Lord, ceasing never to assemble all that has been. And in the Realm of the Dead have ye begotten from the Dead the Shining One. Ye then gave birth and nourished Him.

Thy Land of Milk shall have the honey also, dropped down as dew by the Divine Gynander. The pleasure and delight lies in the Working, the whole surpassing far the Parts together.

The Lord of Parts is placed within His Kingdom, as done by Beast and Bird. The

land of Sun is open but to Children.
Heed the Eternal Child – his Way is flowing-free, and suited to the Nature of
your being.

A Voice crieth in the Crystal Echo,
What means this showing-forth? Is
Time itself awry? The Hawk has flown
but threescore and ten in His allotted
course!

She smiles, as beauteous as Night:
Behold, He spreads His pinions yet in
flight, showering and shaking forth the
Golden Light upon the hearts of men.
And wherein doth He fly, and by what
means? The Feather and the Air are his
to ride, to bear Him ever in His GO-ing.

The pylons of the ages are unshaken, firmly are they Set. The Day of the Hawk has
but seen its dawning, and will see its
due measure according to the Laws of
Time and Space.

The Voice then spoke:
Then has the Vision failed? Do I behold
Thee crookedly, thinking Thee to be Whom
Thou art Not?

She danced and whirled, scattering starlight in her silent laughter.

I am Whom I appear to be, at times, and
then again I wear a triple veil. Be not
confused! Above all, Truth prevails.

I am the Unconfined. Who is there to say
me nay, to say, "Thou shalt not pass"? Who
indeed may say, "Thy time is yet to come,
when Time itself is my chief serving-maid,
and Space the major-domo of my Temple?

Indeed, O Voice of the Akasha, I am the means by which you speak. By the same mouth that breathes the Air, do words of doubt pour forth. In silence, then, do know Me. For I am come with purpose at this time, to aid the Lovers of the Hawk to fly.

The Word of Flight

Who falters in the flight must thereby fall; the greatness of the gods is in the GO-ing.

When first ye fledged, Beloved of Heru, the shell which had protected long had broken. Upon the Wings of Will ye ventured forth, gaining strength and power as ye flew. Ye gained all knowledge of the Feathered Kingdom, whereby ye became as perfect as the Sun. The friends and teachers all became as brothers.

The regal Swan, the Heron and the Owl—the Raven and the Cockerel did aid ye. The Beauty of the Hawk Himself was granted, the virtues of the Peacock, the Hummingbird and Loon. The Eagle did reveal her inner nature and the Mysteries thereof — behold, ye witnessed how, with her Lion, she became the Swan. And the Ibis of the Abyss did show the Knowledge.

Ye flew, O Kings and Hermits! And ye fly even now, within the bending looliness of NU. But there are those among ye, and below ye, who would snare your wings and drag ye from the sky!

Look well within! Judge well your Heart! If ye be pure, it weighs no more than I. It will not bear ye down to

the Abyss. For Gold is Light; but Lead is fatal unto flying – plumb your own depths; in Truth and in Self-knowledge.

If aught would hinder thee, it is thy doing. Behold this teaching now within the Temple.

So saying, She-Who-Moves assumed the form of the great Black Flame, growing from the central shaft and billowing out into the Void. The Children of Heru beheld in silence, and listened to Her words form in their hearts.

Behold! This lens of Stars now turning in Space before ye – men have named it well Andromeda. Through it I flow unto the holy Moondog, and thence to Ra, and thence to ye, O Priests.

Ye must not rest content whilst in the Kingdom, but strive and so exceed in what is done. In Love of the Lady of the North, and in Will of the Prince of the South, do every thing soever. In the power of the Seven-rayed Star do ye comprehend the Beast. And from HAD of the Heart do delight in thy star-arched darling.

Do all this, and then, pass, beyond. Abandon aught that might distinguish thee from any other thing, yea, or from no-thing. If the fowler would snare thee, leave thy feather-cloak a-dangle in his hand and soar naked and invisible beyond!

But now! As priests within the Temple are ye here, as Kings, and Warriors, Magicians all. The Way is in the Work.

The Hidden One of the Abyss now gives

the two wherein is wrought the Higher
Alchemy: supporting Earth is Chthonos –
learn it well, and all bonds shall be
loosed for the Will's Working. Surmounting Spirit, there is Ychronos, whose
nature is duration and the passing –
away thereof.

The two are one, and form the Kingdom's
essence. Who masters them is Master of
the World. They are the utter keys of
Transmutation, and keys of the power
of other Elements.

The Warrior Priests received the keys,
and placed them within their robes; To
hold them hidden well above their hearts.
The Black Flame danced and dwindled,
becoming small, a quill pen, plumed
and pointed. There being naught upon
which to write, one among the Priests
came forth, and laid his body's skin
upon the altar as living parchment.

She-Who-Moves wrote thereupon a Word,
but shew it not before them. In patience
waited all the Kings and Hermits, assured
full well of final Understanding.

The Feather grew again, and rounded
close its edges, becoming to their eyes the
Yonilignam. The image came of Ancient
Baphomet, the Hornéd One, who spoke:

Of old ye knew the Key of Two-in-One
conjoined. Ye have lived and loved full
measure as NU and HAD, as PAN and
BABALON. The Mystery of mine own image
do ye also know, for such a Truth was
for the ancient Orders of the East and West.

Bipartate has the Race of Man been in
its span. The Father and the Mother made
a Child. I am the elder of the Children,
true – but now the younger rises to His
Day.

The nature of true Alchemy is that it changes not alone the substance of the Work, but also changes thence the Alchemist. Ye whose Will it is to Work thereby, behold mine inverse image, and consider well its meaning for thy Task.

The Showing of the Image

From out the Yonilignam drifted forth a cloud, violet and light-shot. In the misty heart thereof, a sound arose, vibrating soft, yet filling everywhere.

Jewlled and flashing, rainbow-lights from wings, there hovered in the midst an humble BEE. Striped gold and brown, soft-haired and curved in form, it shone its eyes unto the Priests and Kings assembled

Spoke then She-Who-Moves from out the mist surrounding:

This is the symbol of the Work-to-come. The Great Glyrander in its earthly form. The Magickian shall grow like unto the BEE as the Aeon unfolds, a leader and a sign unto the Race of Man.

What then of its nature doth the BEE show forth?

Behold, it is not male nor female in the singular. It labors forth by day in constant flight, an ego-less do-er, whose Will and the Hive-Will are but one.

It gathers up the flower-nectar, flies to Hive, and there, in pure Comm-Union, doth in its very body Transubstantiate.

The Nectar is now Honey. Bee to bee, it is transferred, speaking all Hive Mysteries from and to each mouth. By the same mouth that first ingathered, is the Honey spent, the secret Alchemy within the

Centres turning Silver — Gold.

The Hive now lives, immortal. With queen and workers. drones and builder-bees, soldiers, fostermothers - all are one. In constant life-renewal the Hive breathes as One Being - for so indeed it is. In the Will of the Hive is the Will of the Bee fulfilled. Each in its appointed place, the Bees work out their Will in ordered harmony.

The image fades. Now the poised plume moves in dancing fashion, unfolding from the center shaft long wings, transforming to the shape of the dark Vulture.

But know, O Children of the Hawk, a Man is not a Bee. He may profit from the image thereof, to learn of Wisdom in the Working. Behold in Me another image for thy heart's instruction.

There rose before their eyes the Tower of Silence, wherein the Lovers of the Fire lay the dead.

The Vulture form alighted soft therein, and ate the flesh from corpses, to the bone. The wind howled, desolate, in this fearsome place, fluttering the cerements about the ivory bones.

Silently, the Winged One stared, gore smeared about her beak. Into the eyes of each Priest there assembled, her baleful gaze did search. In perfect peace did they behold her searching, for each, as Warrior, had made of Death a brother. Deliberately, then, she unfolded out her wings, and took to the wind, and soared up from that place.

* * * * * * * *

The Giving of the Word

Eternity then reigned. Infinite the veil that hung about them.

Somewhere, sometime, the veil parted for a moment, and She-Who-Moves strode forth. More comely than mortal woman ever was, She glowed in radience of pearl and amethyst. Fine pleated linen was Her gown, girded in gold and silver, and on Her head, a nemyss of starred blue. Her crown was but a single plume, free-standing, and in Her hands the ankh and Wand of Healing.

Unto each Warrior-Priest she moved, embraced and kissed them. Then, seated in the midst, She spoke as comrade equally-ranked.

"All ye who practise well the High Art, hearken. There shall be nothing hidden from thy sight. All formulae and words shalt thou discover, being initiated by those whose Work it is to aid the Law of Will.

"What was given by Aiwaz is yet unfolding. There is much to do for slaves but newly freed into their Kingship, as ye well know. And each who Works within the Kingdom proceeds apace, according to his Will.

"Ye have worked well in all that has been given—upon the Tree of Life are ye founded. In Tetrogrammaton have ye proceeded; in all the Beast hath given have ye practised well. Ye have become Hadit, and Nu, and Ra-Hoor-Khuit also. As Heru-Pa-Kraath did ye abide in silence. Ye know Pan as lover and as godform, and Babalon is bride and Self to you.

"The forces of Shaitan have ye engendered, calling forth the neµs of the ninety-three to work your Will. Separation for the joy of

76 ~

Union have ye known, and Alchemy is Science to your Art.

"For those who know, and Will, and dare, and keep in silence, it goes now further.

"In death is life – for now as ever has it been so. The Willed Death is eternal – keep it so. Self of Ego, selfson born of Maya, must be slain on the moment of birth. The unsleeping Eye must vigil keep, O Warriors, for the illusion is self-generate.

"Constant watchfulness is the first Act – the Abyss is crossed by minutes, every day.

"If ye would dance the Mask, then mask the Dance. Exquisite must be the Art in this wise; and balance in the Centre be maintained, or else ye shall give unwonted Life unto thine own creations. Tread carefully this path of Working, Mage. A tool, by Will devised, makes an ill master.

"Now in the Mass, the Eagle must be fed upon what she has shared in making. By the same mouth that roars upon the mountain, is the word-act of No Difference given.

"And when Will declares, therein shall join the Bee to add the gold to red and white. The essence of Shaitan is nectar here, the Temple is the Hive. The Lion is the Flower, now betimes, the Eagle invokes the nature of the Bee.

"Within the triple-chambered shrine is the first nectar pooled. The summons of the wand of Pan awakens the portal-opening bliss. And from the third and inmost chamber, in joy supreme, the Sothis-gift, quintessential Mead, bounds forth to join Eagle-tears and Lion-blood.

"Solve et coagula. Comm-Union thereby, whereof the Cosmos itself dissolveth, and re-forms by Will. And know, if aught can be so ordered in the Kingdom, that three or more is zero, as well as older Truths."

Then stirred the Warrior-Priests, and of their number, a nameless one stepped forth.

"We know Thee, Lady, unspoken though Thy name has been thus far. But say now—what was written on the manskin? What is the word Thou givest?"

She smiled and drew from out Her robe a parchment scroll, shaped even as a Star. Unrolling it, She turned it roundabout, so all might see.

IPSOS

"What is this Word, O Lady—how may it be used?"

"In silent wisdom, King and Warrior-Priest. Let the deed shine forth, and let the word be hidden—the deed is lamp enough to veil the face.

"It is the word of the twenty-third path, whose number is fifty and six. It is the unspoken Abode, wherein the Dance of the Mask is taught by Me. Tahuti watches without the Ape; I am the Vulture also.

"It is the Chalice of Air and Wand of Water, the Sword of Earth and Pantacle of Fire. It is the hourglass and tail-biting serpent. It is the Ganges becoming Ocean, the Way of the Eternal Child.

"It names the Source of Mine Own Being—and yours. It is the origin of this sending, that channels through Andromeda and Set. What race of gods do speak to Man, O Willed Ones? The word of them is both the Name and Fact.

"It is for thee mantram and incantation. To speak it is to bring about certain change. Be circumspect in its use-age—for if its truth be known abroad, it would perchance drive the slaves to madness and despair.

"Only a true Priest-King may know it fully, and stay in balance through his GOing flight. This is all I speak for now. The

Book of the Preshadowing of the Feather is complete. Do what thou wilt shall be the whole of the Law. Love is the Law, love under will."

INDEX

HORUS-MAAT LODGE

HorusMaatLodge.com

Made in the USA
Middletown, DE
21 September 2024

61197080R00050